Growing a Christian Family

Welcome to the Family!

For Parents Whose Child Is About to Be Baptized

Richard A. Melheim

CPH.
SAINT LOUIS

Unless otherwise noted, the Scripture quotations in this publication are from *The Holy Bible: NEW INTERNATIONAL VERSION,* © 1973, 1978, 1984 by the International Bible Society. Used by permission of Zondervan Bible Publishers.

Copyright © 1989 Concordia Publishing House
3558 S. Jefferson Avenue, St. Louis, MO 63118-3968
Manufactured in the United States of America

All rights reserved. No part of this publication may be reproduced, stored in a retrieval system, or transmitted, in any form or by any means, electronic, mechanical, photocopying, recording, or otherwise, without the prior written permission of Concordia Publishing House.

Library of Congress Cataloging in Publication Data

---

*To Ray and Kate,
who brought me into God's Family,
and to
Kathryn Elizabeth,
our precious new gift from God.*

Contents

Introduction	7
1. The Greatest Gift You Can Give	9
2. A Birth in the Family	15
What is baptism?	15
Why is baptism necessary?	19
3. Why Baptize Babies?	22
The question of infant baptism	22
The origin of infant baptism	25
4. Two Important Questions	30
How do you do it?	
(The question of immersion)	30
What if it doesn't work?	
(The question of rebaptism)	32
5. Two Tips	35
The sponsors	35
The service	37
6. Baptism: For the Rest of Your Life	39
Letter to Sponsors	45

Introduction

The birth of a child marks a critical passage in the lives of most couples. Marriage and commitment, goals and values, life purpose and self-identity all stand at a challenging crossroad. The future fills with exciting and fearful possibilities as a new character enters the family stage. And no matter how easy or hard the transition into parenthood may seem to the couple, one thing is certain: The new parents' lives will never be the same.

As the curtain rises on this unexplored phase of life, most new parents find themselves critically reexamining their faith along with their values, dreams, and goals. And no matter how many parenting classes they've attended or how many books they've read on the subject, most parents feel a sudden inadequacy and a twinge of helplessness mixed with the joy of bringing that precious bundle home from the hospital. Many find themselves vulnerably admitting their need for help and reaching out for the the first time in years to God, the church, and/or anyone else who will offer guidance and loving support.

At this critical time of questioning and searching, the church has a great opportunity to strengthen and sustain the family's life in meaningful ways. Through the gift of baptism God offers a powerful resource for nurture and growth.

Baptism is God's gift of acceptance and belonging. It is more of a message than a ceremony. In baptism God says to every child: "Welcome to My family. You belong!" To every parent God says: "This child being entrusted to you is My child. Remember that always, and raise him/her to know just who and whose they are!" To some parents God may be using the event of a baptism to say "Welcome back!" and to challenge them to a more active and involved participation in the life of the church. And to every congregation God is saying: "Take care of this precious gift. Do everything in your power to see that he/she grows up to know My love!"

This book is a short study of the meaning, power, acceptance, and grace of Christian baptism. It is written (1) to encourage and challenge new parents to look closely at the meaning of the sacrament for them; (2) to lead parents to explore the gifts God waits to give them and their child through the family of faith; and (3) to help parents through this special time in their lives, leading them toward becoming the best, strongest, most loving models of the Christian life they can possibly be for their child.

1
The Greatest Gift You Can Give

A cry in the night
a child is born
pushed and churned and squeezed and pulled
stolen from the muffled black security of one world
and thrown into the harsh gasping helplessness of another.

Gone is the warmth, the dark subdued quiet
gone the lifeline, the water, the cushioned home
where heartbeat, motion, and silence
enveloped existence in safety.
Pushed and churned and squeezed and pulled
into the blinding foreign brightness,
into the world of piercing noises, of rough hands,
of grasps and gasps of breath
and aloneness.

Some say all of life is a search for the womb,
a race from those who drug us out of the safety,
a journey through the harsh struggles of life and breath
to return and rest at last in the womb of timelessness
with the One who first called us
into being

The Future Is Now

The pain, the push, the grasp, the cry—and suddenly the future is now. Your child is born, and life can no longer be the same. It is apparent. You are a parent. You are no longer your own. A child belongs to you, and you belong to a child.

The pain fades into awe as you realize for the first moment that God has shared with you a glimpse of the Creator's image. You have been part of a miracle. You have been allowed to share in the ecstasy of creation!

You are now a partner with God in a journey that will take you where you've never been before. It is a journey that will bring you to explore your world in a new way, one that will lead you into the depths of your own mind and self.

God has given you a child and has entrusted to you one of the most sacred privileges and responsibilities a human can know. To care for another, to raise another person to adulthood, to bring another human being up to know the meaning of life, of love, and of God's grace—this is your call. And it is as frightening and exciting a call as you'll ever experience.

The World Your Child Will Face

The world that your child will face will be one of change, churning, and wonder. It will be a world vastly different from the one that nurtured your childhood. It will be a world of changing structures and challenged values. Where it has taken hundreds of years to add to the basic pool of knowledge in the sciences, information in this new world is doubling every five years or less. Where you grew up in a world with an economy revolving around production and industry, your child has entered an age that will place more value on information and services. There is a dramatic difference between today's society and the one of your youth. Your child is apt to face pressures and ethical struggles in grade school that you didn't face until high school or beyond.

What kind of a world will your children see as they grow into adolescence? What will be their major struggles as they enter adulthood? What kinds of challenges will today's children encounter as they prepare to start families of their own?

One thing is certain: In these first formative years of your children's lives they need every good resource available to help them grow up to be the strong, loving, caring adults you want them to be. They will need to be equipped in the best ways.

But what can you do to prepare them? What can you give them to assure that they will start out in the right direction? How can you give them the resources to grow into the future and to face it with strength, courage, hope, and faith?

As a new parent you are no doubt as full of questions as you are of joy. You are excited about the beautiful gift God has given you, but you know that it is not going to be easy. You want the best for your child, but you may not be sure where to start. You want to give your child the keys to a life of meaning and fullness, but where can you turn?

The Bible tells us that life finds its greatest meaning and fullness when it is centered on the love of God in the person of Jesus Christ. And that's where the Christian parent starts—with the source of all love.

Baptism: The Beginning

Jesus Christ is the foundation for a life of true love, joy, meaning, and fullness. And baptism is the beginning point of that life with Him.

Christian baptism is the starting point of a *life lived in relationship* with God through Christ. It is the beginning of a life tapped into the greatest resource available to the world. In baptism your child's life is plugged into the source of God's love and power. Your child is adopted into a large and wonderful family and is promised a rich inheritance. Your little one is brought into a caring community that promises to stand by you and with you as you begin the tremendous task of raising a child in this changing world.

Baptism is the starting point of the Christian life. Like the fertilized egg cell that attached itself nine months ago to the mother's womb and found a place to grow, your child's Christian existence begins in baptism as the precious little life is attached to the womb of Christ's body on earth—the church. Within this womb of love and fellowship the new Christian life will find spiritual nourishment and a place to grow. Attached to this womb, your precious child will have a chance to develop and mature, becoming all that God intends him or her to be.

In baptism God *claims* your child and *names* your child. Through water and the Word your child is set aside as belonging to God's family and marked and sealed with the cross of Christ. Through God's grace your child is named an inheritor of all the good gifts the loving Creator has to give. Baptism is the first step in a life-long relationship with God. It is the beginning of the process of growth that can bring a person to find true meaning in love and life.

No Hocus-Pocus

Baptism is not magic. It is not an automatic "fix" or an eternal fire insurance policy that God slips into our back pockets when we aren't looking. Baptism is not a religious ceremony or ritual to guarantee that the child will remain a lifelong Christian. It will not place an aura of protection around your child. It is no guarantee that the child will grow up to be an angel or have a nicer disposition or less messy diapers. Baptism is not a magic spell. It is a gift.

Baptism is a visible sign of God's invisible gift of acceptance, forgiveness, adoption, and love. It is as simple and as complex as that. In the Lutheran church, baptism is understood as a *sacrament:* a special act commanded by Jesus, given with a physical element, and a means by which God gives us grace, acceptance, forgiveness, and love. Baptism is God's totally free gift to us. And yet it comes to parents with some important implications and instructions.

Planting Seeds

In baptism God plants the seeds of faith in a young life. God does the planting, but as the seeds are sown, God assigns the parents the task of being good gardeners. They are to nurture and water the seeds of faith. They are to fertilize and prune the young plants just when they need it. They are to see that the seeds get all the support and protection they need until the day when the new plants can stand by themselves and produce beautiful fruit on their own.

In baptism God attaches the fertilized egg of a new spiritual life with all its wonderful potential to the womb of your marriage. But that's not all that happens. With this gift comes a serious and important responsibility. It is a call and charge for you to take good care of the child, to love and support each other, and to make your home the healthiest environment possible for your child's physical *and* spiritual development.

In baptism God also attaches the fertilized egg of your new family to the womb of the Christian community and calls on the whole church to be a healthy, nourishing environment where your family can grow together to know God's forgiveness, love, and power.

A New Life in Your Hands

God has placed a new life into your hands. You are the best tools to give this new life a meaningful, vital, and loving world and to shape it into a caring, maturing young adult. Through your attitudes, your actions, your words, and your life you will be showing your child what it means to live as God's child. The way you live, love, and interact within your family will shape the person your child grows up to be. Your words and deeds from today on will have a powerful impact on how he or she will grow to look at life, love, families, and God.

You have a tremendous responsibility. You are shaping a human life. And in doing this, you are shaping the world.

God has given you this gift as a trust. At birth God placed your child into the love and care of your family. From that day on, God counts on you to bring the child up to know love, to live love, and to understand what it means to belong to the Creator of the universe. It is an awesome task. But you will not be alone. In baptism God also reminds the members of the whole Christian family that they have a responsibility too. They are to be there for you.

The Greatest Gift

As you looked at that peacefully sleeping little face through the glass window in the hospital on that first night, what was going on in your mind? What were your dreams, hopes, and aspirations? What promises did you make in the depths of your heart for that child? What gifts did you want to give?

The greatest gift you can give your children is to provide a loving, nurturing home where they can grow up to see *in you* an example of the love of their Creator. If your children can come to know the meaning of God's love through you, they will have the strength and resources to make it through all the changes that the future can throw at them. If they see the love and peace of God in you and come to know Jesus through you, they will grow up with a strength and power that will carry them through all their future struggles and decisions. And their lives will have a deeper value and meaning.

This book is a short review of the meaning and fullness that Christian baptism brings. Read it as an investment in the life and future of your child.

Thought Time

What hopes or dreams do you have for your child's future?

What actions can you begin today to help bring these dreams closer to reality?

What promises have you made to yourself or to God since the birth of your child?

What could stop you from keeping those promises?

What is one thing you can do today that will help you to keep those promises?

2

A Birth in the Family

Baptism—
not something we do for God,
but something God does for us.

Claiming us as adopted children
is God's gift to us.
What we do with our lives
is our gift to God.

What Is Baptism?

Baptism is a means by which God's Spirit comes to us to grace our lives with forgiveness, acceptance, and love. The Lutheran church views baptism as a sacrament because it is a special *means of grace* that Christ commanded His disciples to do (Matt. 28:18) and that comes to us connected to a physical element (water).

God is the *initiator* of all the good gifts we receive in this life. God first gives us our lives and a marvelous world in which to live. We don't ask for these gifts. They are simply given out of God's grace. As we grow in years, God gives us the ability to discover, learn, and understand. We don't ask for these abilities. They are simply given as a part of who we are.

God gives us the ability to love. "We love because he first loved us" (1 John 4:19). God even gives us the ability to have faith. "By grace you have been saved through faith—and this not from yourselves, it is a gift of God—not by works, so that no one can boast'' (Eph. 2:8–9). We believe because God creates in us the ability to believe.

All these gifts come to us freely, whether we ask for them or not. God gives. We receive. God gives air. We breathe. God gives life. We live. That's how it works.

God's love and acceptance are not based on our own goodness. They are gifts that come to us whether or not we deserve them. With this in mind—that God is the *initiator* of love, faith, and all good gifts—how can we view the Sacrament of Baptism? What is it?

To answer this question let's look at what Jesus said about Baptism.

The Holy Spirit at Work

In the third chapter of the gospel of John we find Jesus talking about Baptism with Nicodemus. When Jesus said, "You must be born again . . . of water and the Spirit," he was telling Nicodemus that baptism was vital. Baptism isn't just a matter of pouring water over someone. It's more than an admission that we are sinners who need God's forgiveness. According to Jesus, *the Holy Spirit is at work*. Through baptism, the Spirit gives us new life and brings us into the kingdom of God.

In a similar way, the apostle Paul reminded the Corinthians that baptism was the means *the Holy Spirit* used to make them members of Christ's body, the church (1 Cor. 12:13). Paul makes it plain that baptism is far more than a rite of initiation. God works through baptism, bringing us together, uniting us with his Son, and blessing us with His Holy Spirit.

We know that God creates us and gives us the gift of life before we can prove we are worthy of it. We do nothing to initiate it. We simply receive it. Our responsibility in life is our *response* of thanks and praise for the marvelous gift God has given.

Likewise, Christ died for us while we were sinners—before we even had faith. He didn't say to us, "First be good enough and then I'll love you." By His life and death He simply said, "I love you and want to save you regardless of who you are or what you've done." Our responsibility in faith is not to make salvation happen. We simply respond to what God has already done for us. God gives. We receive. God loves. We love in return. God accepts us. We accept our acceptance. God acts. We react to that action.

And that's how it works in baptism!

This is the most important point to be made about Christian baptism: *God is the active force*. God is doing the giving. God is doing the accepting. As with all the rest of God's good gifts, we do not initiate God's gift of acceptance in baptism. We simply receive it. And later as we grow to know and understand that God has accepted us, we grow in our appreciation of His grace. First we receive. Then we believe.

An Invitation and a Key

Baptism is God's statement of love, acceptance, and forgiveness for a child. But it is also *an invitation to a life lived in relationship*. It is the beginning point of a lifelong process. It is a call to get started in a life of forgiveness. It is a call to live in relationship with the living God every day of our lives. It is a call to a daily dying of the old sinful ways in which a person lives life. It is a call to a daily rising to the new loving existence that God enables us to experience. It is a call to a daily cleansing from our sins. It is a call to a daily walk with Christ.

The key word here is *daily*. And that is where the parents of a child come in again. That is where you have a tremendously important role to play. A child who is to grow up knowing what a living relationship with the living God really means must see it in *your* life. A child who is to grow up knowing what caring, sharing, sacrifice, and Christian values are must come to understand them through your example. If forgiveness and love are going to mean anything to your child, they must be clearly evident in your life. If God is going to mean anything to your child, your words and actions must clearly show that God means something to you.

If your child is going to know Christ and all His fullness, then you as parents must be intimately involved in the process. You are God's best tools in the nurture of your child's life. And you are God's best tools in the nurture of your child's faith. You are God's best hope! If the seeds that are planted on the day of the baptismal ceremony are going to grow, God will be counting on you to do much of the watering that will make it happen!

An Opportunity

Your child's baptism provides you with a great opportunity. It will be a very important day in his/her life. It can also be an especially meaningful event in *your* life and marriage. For in baptism God is not only calling the child. God is also calling you.

Baptism is a call for your child to begin a new life in God's family. But in a broader sense it is also a call for you to commit yourselves to your child at a deeper spiritual level. It is a call for you to recommit yourselves to God so that you can become the most loving, supportive, and caring parents possible. And it is a call for you to recommit yourselves to your marriage so that your home can be the warmest, most loving and nurturing environment possible.

As Christians we believe that God is the source of all love. If our homes, our marriage, our lives are to be filled with love, they must be filled with the presence of God. Living in an awareness of God is living in an awareness of love. Living apart from God is living with less love, less strength, less peace, and less joy than you were meant to know. God is love. Apart from God your child will never know love's true meaning.

Why Is Baptism Necessary?

The Bible teaches us that we are born as children of a fallen humanity. We are not perfect beings. We are born into a broken, sinful world. As humans, we cannot escape being a part of that sinfulness. We are born with original sin (Ps. 51:5).

Sin separates us from our world, from our God, and from ourselves. If we live with sin continually dominating our lives, we will never know the fullness, joy, and strength that God intends for us to experience. We will never find peace with our world, ourselves, or our God. We will never know eternal life.

In Rom. 6:23 Paul tells us that "the wages of sin is death." That's bad news. Unless we can find an escape from our sin, we will pay for it with our lives. This is serious business! Unless we can escape from sin's power, it will destroy us and everything good around us.

The Good News

But there is also good news: In baptism God destroys the power of sin by joining us to the death and resurrection of Jesus Christ. Through baptism the old self with all its sin and rebellion is drowned and buried. As Paul writes, "We were therefore buried with him through baptism into death in order that, just as Christ was raised from the dead through the glory of the Father, we too may live a new life" (Rom. 6:4).

Baptism is a sacrament of newness. It is the beginning of a life in Christ in which the old sinful self is washed clean by the power of God's forgiveness, claimed as God's child, called to live as a new person daily, and made an inheritor of eternal life.

How does this happen? Is there a magic incantation or some hocus-pocus at the ceremony that does all this? Does the ritual automatically save a person's eternal soul? After all, the Bible says that "baptism . . . saves you" (1 Peter 3:21).

If baptism was simply magic, all we would have to do is

bring a child to the font, go through the motions, get it over with, and leave the church—never to return. Some people treat it that way. Some people are foolish and ignorant.

To treat baptism this way is to portray a simplistic and uninformed understanding of it. *For although God gives the child all the benefits of baptism on the day of the ceremony, those benefits are received only through faith. And the faith that is given at baptism must be nurtured if it is to stay alive and keep growing in the life of your child.*

As children grow up in the family of God and hear the word of the Gospel, they learn to know God, to love God, and to trust God for strength, peace, and joy. They begin to understand Christ's sacrificial love and start to live in His forgiveness and newness. This adds a beauty, depth, and power to life that no other experience can equal. Unless children are brought up in a *living relationship* with God, these meaningful benefits just aren't part of their experience, and they miss out on their best chance for a full Christian life.

The Parent's Calling

In Eph. 6:4 God calls all parents to raise their children in a loving atmosphere of Christian discipline and instruction. As children come to know God's will and Word in such surroundings, the Holy Spirit works in their lives to create the full, meaningful relationship with God that sin has taken from us all. If this wonderful relationship is to develop, your child will need plenty of models of faith, examples of right living, and environments of care and acceptance in which to grow.

Alone, you can't begin to supply all your child's needs or meet this challenge. But if you are committed to the life God wants for you, committed to each other and your task, and committed to your child's Christian development, the Spirit will give you all the tools you need to care for the precious seeds of faith in your children until the day when they can grow on their own.

Thought Time

What qualities do you prize highly in people and want your child to have?

What can you do to teach your child these attributes?

Why is God described as ''the active force'' in Christian baptism?

What call is God giving to the parents in Christian baptism?

What part do the people of the church play in your child's baptism?

3

Why Baptize Babies?

A well-meaning friend comes up to you and tells you that you are wrong to baptize your children until they are old enough to make a choice to be Christians. "Unless they know what is going on and make a conscious choice to follow Christ, baptism isn't valid," the friend says.

How do you answer this friend?

The Question of Infant Baptism

To answer any questions about baptism, it is important for you to remember that baptism is *God's gift of acceptance and forgiveness*. God is the initiator of life, of love, and of faith. To assume that God cannot accept a child unless the child first accepts God is to place the responsibility for faith in the wrong court. God is the lover. "We love because he first loved us" (1 John 4:19). God is the actor. We react to God's love. God takes the responsibility for accepting us. We respond to that acceptance. To assume that a child should not be baptized is to assume that *we* do the acting in baptism—*not God*.

But God *is* the one who acts in baptism. His Spirit is at work, washing away our sins, giving us new life, and making us part of his family. These are gifts we want for our children as well as for ourselves. Thank God he gives them even to infants.

The question of infant baptism has been debated for hundreds of years and has divided branches of the Christian faith. Since you have entered a partnership with God in the creation of this new life, it is important that you understand the Biblical basis for the sacramental gift God is about to give in baptism. You can then come to the font with a clear, informed understanding of the sacrament, and it will begin immediately to make a positive impact on your child's life.

Some branches of Protestantism argue that babies should not be baptized because they are too young to believe. They say that a person has to choose to follow Christ first and then be baptized; otherwise baptism isn't real. The Bible's answer to this logic is clear: God's power is not limited by our faith—or lack of it. God's power in baptism is not dependent on the child's cooperation. God's power creates faith in all of us, whether young or old. (Remember Eph. 2:8—"By grace you have been saved, through faith—and this not from yourselves, it is the gift of God.")

Lazarus: From Death to Life

When Jesus raised Lazarus from the dead, did the faith of Lazarus make him alive (John 11:38–44)? No. It wasn't his faith or actions that saved him. It was the grace-filled word of God from the lips of Christ: "Lazarus, come out!" God spoke, and Lazarus was made alive. He had no part in it. It was as simple and as complex as that.

Do people have to know exactly what is going on and to believe for God to be able to work in their lives? Lazarus had been dead for three days when Christ acted on his behalf.

Naaman the General

When the Syrian general Naaman asked the prophet Elisha to heal him of his leprosy, Elisha told him to wash in a dirty river. Naaman laughed at Elisha and didn't believe that it would do him any good. But he finally did what he was told, scoffing all the way. And to his surprise, he was healed (2 Kings 5:1–14).

Must a person have a living faith for God to be able to

act on his or her behalf? Naaman laughed and doubted up to the moment of his miracle.

The Spirit Goes Where It Wills

It is clear from these and countless other Biblical stories that God is not limited to working only where there is great faith. Although some of Christ's miracles are attributed to the strong faith of the individuals healed, the Bible shows us many other examples from our Lord's life in which His power worked for good in spite of people's shallow faith.

Look up the following verses and ask how God worked apart from people's faith in each case:

Matt. 15:21–28	Jesus heals a girl through her mother's faith.
Matt. 15:32–39	Jesus miraculously feeds 4,000 people when not even the disciples believed.
Luke 8:40–56	Jesus brings a dead girl back to life even though the parents and friends disbelieve.
John 11:1–44	Jesus brings Lazarus to life by His word of power.

The people in these examples had little or nothing to do with initiating Christ's life-giving miracles. It was the power of God's Word that brought life. God spoke and it happened.

God's Powerful Word

The Genesis creation account uses two different Hebrew words to paint a poetic contrast between God's creation of the universe and of the human race. *Bara* is used for the creation of the heavens and the earth. *Bara* means to call into being or to create something from nothing. God speaks and it happens.

Yatzer means to form or mold something, as a potter molds a lump of clay. When God called the human race into being, the word *yatzer* was used. It gives us the picture of God laboring like a master potter, working in the mud to form and mold us into the Creator's own image.

And that is how it is with baptism. First God calls something from nothing. God speaks, and through the water and the Word we are claimed as children. We are God's. We belong. Then as the years pass, God uses our parents, sponsors, and the Christian community to be the hands that mold and shape us into the loving, caring, faithful Christian people we were meant to be. *Baptism calls faith into being.* It is the beginning. Shaping and growth are the goal.

Think of the responsibility a parent has! You are God's "molding hands." God is trusting you!

But Can God Create Faith in a Child?

Some say that God cannot work in the heart of a child until the child is old enough to think and understand. What does the Bible say about this? In Matt. 18:6 Jesus indicated that little children really did believe in Him. Their faith was precious in His sight. He used a child's faith as a model for the faith that adults should have. In Luke 1:41 the Holy Spirit was working in John the Baptist's life even before he was born; he jumped in his mother's womb at the news of the conception of Jesus. God told Jeremiah, "Before I formed you in the womb I knew you" (Jer. 1:5). Jeremiah was called to be God's prophet even before he was born!

And some say that God cannot work in the life and faith of a child! There's news for those folks. The Bible says that God can work in the little life even before birth.

The Origin of Infant Baptism

How would you answer a friend who said, "Show me just one place in the Bible where it says that babies should be baptized and I will believe in infant baptism"?

The Roots

Jesus said nothing about the age at which a person was to be baptized. He baptized no one Himself, as far as we know. But He did give His disciples a clear and distinct command before He ascended into heaven. He told them, "Go and make disciples of all nations, baptizing them in the name of the Father and of the Son and of the Holy Spirit, and teaching them to obey everything I have commanded you" (Matt. 28:19–20).

Baptizing all nations—that was Christ's final command. He said nothing about baptizing only certain groups. His instructions were simply to go and do it.

Since we don't hear a specific word about who should be baptized from the lips of Jesus, we must use the rest of the Bible and the practices of the disciples who sat at Jesus' feet to get an idea of Christ's intentions.

The Early Church

From what we can tell of the early church, the apostles baptized both adults and children. They went from city to city, and when a group of people heard the powerful story of Jesus and were moved to believe, the entire group was baptized into the faith.

Look up these passages and note how they relate to the question of infant baptism.

Acts 2:37–41 During Peter's sermon at Pentecost he told the people that the promise was "for you and your children."

Acts 16:14–15 Lydia heard the word and became a worshiper of God. She and "the members of her household" were baptized. Most families in those days had several children. The Bible does not say that all but the children were baptized. The whole family was involved.

Acts 16:33   The Philippian jailer heard what Christ had done and believed it, and that night "he and all his family were baptized."

1 Cor. 1:16   Paul baptized the "household of Stephanas."

The catacombs of Rome bear inscriptions and drawings that document baptisms of adults, children, and infants during the early years of the persecution. From the Bible's record and historical church writings of the first century it is clear that children were included in the family of God through baptism from the beginning. The apostles of Jesus had no problem with baptizing children.

The Key

The disciples did not go about indiscriminately grabbing babies off the streets to baptize them and thus to save their immortal souls through the simple participation in a ceremony. The key to infant baptism in the first century was a community of faith. The key was a Christian family where the young seeds of faith could be planted and find a place to sprout and grow into mature young Christians.

There have been times in the history of the faith when overzealous and uninformed Christians have abused infant baptism. With a simplistic and irresponsible understanding of the sacrament, they have taken babies from the arms of objecting mothers and plunged them under water, thinking that they were doing their Christian duty and performing the child an eternal favor.

This was a gross error. Baptism does not save us on the basis of a magical or ritual symbolic act. *Baptism saves because of God's promise*. Through God's promise in baptism the Holy Spirit plants the seeds of faith within a child—a faith that is intended to grow. And that's where the parents and sponsors come in again.

It would be superstitious and totally irresponsible for parents to think that they could bring their child to be baptized and leave it at that. A child's baptism day is the day when God plants the seeds of faith in the child's life. And it is the day when God says to the parents, "Go! See that you take good care of these precious seeds. Water them. Nurture them. Raise them up to produce good things. You are my gardeners. I'm counting on you!"

This is an awesome responsibility. But the parents are not alone in the venture. God's Spirit promises to be with them every step of the way.

Jesus Accepted Children

Jesus had some clear words about the place of children in the family of God. He didn't shun them or put them down for their simplistic faith. In fact, He told the adults around Him, "Unless you change and become like little children, you will never enter the kingdom of heaven" (Matt. 18:3). Jesus scolded those who chased the little ones away from Him: "Let the little children come to me, and do not hinder them, for the kingdom of God belongs to such as these" (Mark 10:14). Jesus apparently had more faith in the faith of children than in that of many adults.

When Nicodemus came to Him at night (John 3:1–21), Jesus told the respected member of the Jewish council that there was no way to enter heaven except by being "born again," "born of the water and the Spirit" (vv. 3, 5). He did not say that heaven comes to those who through their own rational adult understanding and intellect come to God. Instead, it was necessary to become like a child in the faith in order to find the kingdom.

From the words of Jesus it is clear that intellect and understanding do not save us or assure us a place in the kingdom of God. It is God's Spirit who gives us the gift of eternal life. Clearly this is God's doing, not our own. Our part is simply to accept that we have been accepted, to believe in the love and forgiveness our God has for us in Jesus Christ, and to live as the people God created us to be.

Whose Doing?

In summary, if Christian baptism is only for those who have enough faith to repent and believe, we are wrong and hypocritical to baptize anyone who is too young to exhibit these qualities. But the Bible clearly shows that God is the initiator of faith. And since faith, forgiveness, and acceptance are God's doing—not our own—we simply must follow Christ's command to baptize and teach. We must not put limits on God or try to dictate who God can love and accept as a child of the kingdom. We simply do as Christ commanded and trust in Him for the rest.

Can our Creator plant the seeds of faith in a child? If the answer is yes, it is a wonderful miracle of grace. If the answer is no, then God is not as powerful as the Bible indicates.

Thought Time

What examples from Jesus' words show His attitude toward the faith of children?

How would you now answer a friend who thought that you were wrong to have your baby baptized?

Look at parts 1 and 2 of the explanation of Holy Baptism in Luther's Small Catechism. According to Luther, why do we baptize children?

4

Two Important Questions

How Do You Do It?

As you talk about baptism with your friends and acquaintances, you may run into people who sincerely believe that baptism is only valid if it is done by immersion—submerging the person totally under water. Immersing is indeed a good symbolic act. It represents a total washing, a dying of the old and a rising to the new life in Christ. "That's the way that Jesus did it," they'll say. And although it doesn't say this explicitly in the Bible, it was a tradition for Jewish baptism.

How can we answer this question? First, it is important to know that the verb "to baptize" (*baptizein*) in the Greek texts has seven different meanings. *Baptizein* is used for "to pour, to dip repeatedly, to immerse, to submerge, to wash, to sprinkle," and "to cleanse with water." The word did not refer to only one kind of action in the early church; it covered many.

In Acts 2:37–41 we find Peter preaching at Pentecost and moving people to see their need for Christ and His forgiveness. The Bible says that 3,000 people were baptized that day. Immersion was almost impossible there. The nearest river was many miles away. Acts 9:18–19 suggests that Paul was baptized in a home in Damascus. Total immersion in his case was unlikely.

The Roman caverns and catacombs (where the early Christians worshiped during times of persecution) have well-preserved drawings and paintings that show a variety of baptismal practices. Some picture baptism by sprinkling, others by pouring water on the head, and others show immersion. The method was not important to the early Christians. Only in the last 450 years have the specifics become a matter of concern. Beginning the new life in Christ is what mattered to the early Christians, not how much water was used. That's what mattered most to them then, and that's what should matter the most to us now.

According to Paul, "all of you who were baptized into Christ have clothed yourselves with Christ" (Gal. 3:27). Putting on Christ and receiving Him into our hearts is what counts, not the amount of water placed on our heads.

Who Is Acting in Baptism?

From the earliest of Christian tradition it is clear that *immersion, sprinkling, and pouring water on the head were all used.* Yet some today say that baptism is only valid if the person is totally submerged.

This brings us back to the main question. Who is doing the acting in baptism anyway? Is it our acting to please God, or is it God acting on our behalf? If baptism is our action, then we'd better do the ceremony exactly right or the "magic" might not work. But if baptism is God's acting for us, then God can certainly work apart from any ceremonial foul-ups or blunders on the part of mere humans.

What is important in baptism is that God is acting through the water with the Word to claim us as children. It is not merely our symbolic dedication of a child to God. It is God saying through water and the Word, "This child is Mine!" The validity of the sacrament does not depend on how well we perform a ceremony—on what we do. It depends on what God does. It is God's gift.

The Bible does not say whether we should use a thimbleful, a bucketful, or a whole river of water for baptism. This is not important. What is important is that the Word of God and water are used as Christ commanded; that we do it in the name of the Father, Son, and Holy Spirit; and that we follow up by teaching the child to know Christ.

What If It Doesn't Work the First Time?

If a baptized person grows up and falls away from God, is it necessary for that person to be rebaptized in order to reenter the Christian community?

When I was in high school, a friend of mine who had left the Christian community for a time finally got his life straightened out. He deeply desired to show God and the rest of his friends that he wanted to return to Christ. He prayed and asked Christ to forgive him and come into his heart. But some sincere Christians who had befriended him said that that wasn't enough. He would not be considered a "real Christian" unless he was rebaptized.

What would *you* say to someone who told you that you needed to be rebaptized?

Back to the Question

The answer to this problem goes back to the main questions of our study: "What exactly is baptism?" and "Who is acting in baptism anyway?" If the validity of baptism depends on the faith of the person being baptized, then rebaptism might at times become necessary. Our faith might someday fail us.

But Christian baptism rests on the sure promises of God. If it is performed according to God's command and promise, it is valid and remains so forever. Since baptism is God's acting on behalf of the person, planting the seeds of faith and adopting the person into the family of Christ, then who are we to say to God, "God, you didn't do it right the first time. It didn't 'take,' and so the baptism has to be done again"?

What Is Baptism?

If Christian baptism is not something we do for God, then what is it? In 1 Cor. 12:13 we find baptism described as the Holy Spirit grafting us into the body of Christ. The Holy Spirit is the active agent, not the person being baptized.

If there ever comes a time in your life when you feel that you have left or forgotten God—if there comes a time when you see your sins and feel a need to repent and return to your loving Creator—you can do just that! Repent of your sin. Pray for forgiveness. Ask the Spirit to strengthen and renew you and to lead you to live in God's will. But don't be so presumptuous as to say that God didn't do it right the first time and that you have to be baptized again! If you find yourself far from God, it wasn't God who moved. You may have given up on the Lord at a trying time in your life, but God has never given up and will never give up on you.

You were claimed as God's child long ago. And God will not let go of that claim.

Reaffirming the Relationship

Lutherans believe that reaffirming baptismal vows in later life is necessary. This may happen at a confirmation service. It may happen out in the woods at a Bible camp. It may happen a number of times in your life as you are continually drawn to see the marvelous beauty of Christ's sacrificial love and come to the realization of your need for forgiveness and restoration. Luther wrote that we should *daily* repent of the old sinful self and ask God to create new hearts in us so that we can live for Christ afresh each day. "Drown your sins daily," Luther said, "so that every day a new person can arise to serve God."

In baptism God writes us a check. As we confirm our faith and go to God daily for newness, we endorse the check and begin to draw out the marvelous benefits in our lives again and again.

Thought Time

How would you answer a person who told you that your baptism wasn't valid unless you were totally immersed?

How would you answer a person who told you that you had to be rebaptized?

Look at parts 1 and 3 of Luther's explanation of Holy Baptism in the Small Catechism. What constitutes Christian baptism according to Luther? What makes a baptism valid?

5

Two Tips

The Sponsors

Some people put more thought into choosing a household cleanser than they do into choosing baptismal sponsors. Too often this responsibility is taken lightly and given to whoever happens to be conveniently close at the time or to a relative who lives far away and can't often be around to help the child grow.

Before choosing your sponsors, look first at your friends and family members who are worshiping, active Christians. It makes no sense at all to ask someone to be a praying, worshiping witness of God's love to your child if that person doesn't think enough of God to worship regularly.

When asking a person or couple to sponsor your child, first share your thoughts about the commitment involved in baptismal sponsorship. Ask them if they would honestly be able to make the following commitment to your child:

1. **To pray for your child regularly**
2. **To remember your child's baptismal anniversary and birthday every year with a card or letter**
3. **To be a model of love, care, and Christlike kindness**
4. **If any thing should happen to you, to see to it that the child is brought up in the Christian faith, taught to read the Bible as a source of life and direction, and brought to worship regularly.**

You may wish to send the sample letter in the back of this book to your prospective sponsors. Give the information to the people you consider to be your best candidates for sponsorship. Let them take a few days to think about the commitment before asking them for a decision. If they can't make this kind of commitment, thank them for their honesty and find someone else. Your child deserves more than token sponsors who merely stand up in front of the congregation making promises they don't intend to keep.

This may sound harsh and judgmental, but with something as important as your child's life and growth in faith at stake, sponsorship cannot be taken lightly. If you have no friends or relatives who can make this commitment living near enough, ask your pastor to suggest an older couple in your church who might be willing to serve as special prayer partners—"grand-godparents"—for your child.

Baptism, Teaching, and Growth

Baptism and teaching go hand in hand. This is one reason that parents, sponsors, and the whole congregational family speak up on behalf of your child and promise their support. When Jesus commanded baptism in Matthew 28, the word *teach* came in the same breath. To support one without the other (baptism without teaching or vice versa) is to miss the point of both.

As stated before, baptism is not magic. It is not a heavenly fire insurance policy that God slips into your pocket when you aren't looking. It is God's action of adopting you, of claiming you as children. But it is only the beginning of a life meant to be lived in relationship. It is the planting of the seeds of faith that need to be nurtured. And that is where the parents come in again. Baptism is not a ticket to heaven. It is the beginning of a life with God here and now. It is the start of a living relationship.

Seeds in the Garden

You couldn't expect to plant a garden, leave it alone for

four months, and then stroll in to harvest a crop at the end of the summer. All you would get would be a patch of weeds. A garden needs care. It needs water, weeding, protection, nutrients, and pruning.

So it is with a child. You can't expect to baptize a child and then to leave that child to go it alone spiritually. A child needs spiritual nurture just as much as physical needs must be met. To deny a child this aspect of life is a cruel and thoughtless act. No loving parent would willingly set a child up for such an empty, hollow life. Loving parents want their children to have the best resources for life. A good parent would not think of giving birth and then setting the child out on the street to fend for itself. The child would die in a short time.

To bring a child to baptism without following up on the sacrament by feeding the child with the necessary spiritual food (God's Word, prayer, Christian fellowship, the Lord's Supper) is to neglect a parent's duties and to break the baptismal promise. To starve a child spiritually and leave him or her to walk life's dangerous road alone is truly a cruel act. What parent would willingly do this?

You are a new parent. You love and want the best for your child. Be sure that the best begins with a caring set of sponsors who will take their baptismal promises seriously and do all they can to see that your child grows up in the love and knowledge of the Lord.

The Service

Whenever possible, ask that your child's baptism take place during a regular worship service of your congregation. It only makes sense to have as many of the "family" members present as possible to witness the event. Their care, prayers, and support for your child will begin in a special way on that day and become a valuable resource for you in the future if the members of the congregation take their responsibility seriously. Don't let them miss out on this family event. And don't let your child miss out on their love and support.

Private baptisms may be done in emergency cases. But if private baptisms become the norm in a church, the congregation is robbed of the privilege of celebrating the event, and the child is robbed of the prayers, concern, and promise of a committed church.

Note: If you have a hand in choosing or drawing up a special order of service, be sure that the congregation is a full participant in it in some way. The people should not just be a group of spectators. Invite the children to come forward and take part. Write special prayers, blessings, or readings for those assembled. Use your creativity and make it a family event that won't be forgotten.

Thought Time

What three persons or couples would you consider asking to be sponsors for your child?

Which of these could you count on to take the promises of sponsorship seriously?

Write a short prayer or blessing that you would like the congregation to use at your child's baptismal service. You may wish to include a promise by the people to pray for, love, and nurture your child in a special way. Give it to your pastor and ask that it be made a part of the service.

6
Baptism:
For the Rest of Your Life

*"The wedding is a service,
but the marriage is
for the rest of your life."*

If a man and woman get married and then walk out the church door to live separate lives, what is their marriage worth? If they rarely meet or speak—never share their dreams, their joys, their sorrows, or their bed—it can't be considered much of a marriage. You could show a certificate to prove that they were married. But you couldn't show a marriage. Marriage requires a loving, steady relationship. If there is no relationship, there is no marriage.

Baptism is much the same. At the baptism of your child a ceremony is also performed. As in marriage, the meaning of the ceremony only begins with the church service. The ceremony begins a new relationship that is intended to be lived and explored and discovered throughout the rest of life. It is not finished when the parents and child leave the church. It has only begun!

A Parent's Impact

No matter how you might feel later in life—no matter what others may tell you or how out of control your children may seem during adolescence—*you* (the parents) will have the most powerful and lasting impact on your children's lives. You will be *the* shaping force. Even with the tremendous peer pressure that children face during the teen years, parents are still by far the most important influence children will ever know. They will learn from you. They will be molded by you. And they will grow up to become more like you than you will ever know. (They may become more like you than you would ever like them to be!)

In recent years infant psychologists have amazed us with studies showing just how much children pick up from their parents in the first few years (and even months) of life. The basic psychological makeup of a child—the attitudes, personality traits, disposition, and fundamental outlook on the world—is being shaped and molded even before birth. And much of it is based on how the child relates to his or her environment—mainly you!

This is both exciting and frightening for parents to think about. From the moment you first take them out of the nurse's arms, the security you show, the nurture you give, the way you react to problems and respond to your world are shaping and molding your children into the people they will become. The way you treat your mate and the way you treat yourself will be observed and absorbed. It is as if you now have a little spy in your house, and that spy has the mind of a sponge. Little you do will go unnoticed. Your nervous or relaxed attitude, your touch, your voice, your whole state of being are influencing the creation of your child.

If you've been looking for a reason to start your life over in a more purposeful, positive, loving, and trusting direction, this is the best reason you will ever find.

And now is the time to begin. If you want to give your child the best, most secure outlook on life, it must start with the way you live your own. If you react to problems by becoming fearful, edgy, irritable, or worried, you are telling your child how to relate to the world. If you are prayerful, relaxed, confident, hopeful, pleasant, and faithful—even in the most trying times—you are building these attitudes into the life of your child.

What attitudes do you want your child to have? Will the way you are living right now ensure this?

A Different Kind of Promise

You stand before an altar and make a pledge to God on only a few occasions in your life—confirmation, marriage, baptism. Most of these promises are made in earnest. Yet so many are broken almost before the ink is dry on the certificate. In both confirmation and marriage you make the promises for yourself. You stand before God and the congregation and proclaim your intentions of faithfulness in your relationship from that day on. If the relationship breaks down, if you don't fulfill your promises, it is *your* problem. You are the one who must pay the consequences. And you take that responsibility.

But in the baptism of your child, you have a much different situation. You are making promises on behalf of someone else. And if you break these promises, your children will pay the price. They will pay by being deprived of life in all it's fullness. They will pay by missing out on a meaningful relationship with God. They will not come to know the joy and peace of trusting in the loving Creator.

No parent would intentionally steal resources like God's strength, peace, power, and eternal life from a child. Yet so many get so caught up in the busyness of life that the promises are routinely forgotten, and many children are cheated by their own parents out of their best opportunity to grow into loving, caring, confident Christian people.

Half of the marriage vows today are made and broken. The vows meant something at one time, but the commitment wasn't strong enough to withstand the pressures of life. The promises gave way. Even greater percentages of confirmation promises are made and broken—promises of active participation in the worship of God, promises of living in communion with Christ, promises of serving the church and world in love.

Will the promises you make before God and the congregation on the day of your child's baptism be made and broken?

Will you stand before the altar of the almighty God, who created your child within you, and recite a set of vows that you don't intend to keep? It is a fact of our nature that we all fail and fall short of our best intentions from time to time. But with something as important and serious as your child's life, growth, happiness, and eternal destiny at stake, can you afford to take your promises of nurture and faithful witness lightly?

Look at the promises you are making in your child's baptismal service. (They are found in your church worship book.) You are promising faithfully to bring your child to worship—not just to drop the child off at the door. You are promising to make the Bible and its meaning a natural part of your child's life and growth—not just something that sits on a shelf. You are promising to teach the child the basics of the Christian faith—not just to leave that to the Sunday school. You are promising to be the best model of a Christlike life you can be so that your child grows up to know the joy of celebrating a marvelous life in the presence of our loving Creator.

Do you honestly promise to fulfill these obligations? Be careful with your answer. If you say, "I do," you are making a commitment for the rest of your life.

A Final Thought

This is a time of commitment to the total love and growth of your child. In a real sense you are committing yourselves to do all that is in your power to open the child's mind to see the love of God active in the world through its activity in your life. *You are the first, the best, the most credible model for your child.* Through your own loving Christian life, through your example of words and deeds, through your steady, patient, and positive witness, through your life of prayer, worship, and Christian service, you will be doing more to shape your child's image of God than all the preachers and teachers he or she will ever know.

God gave you this child to raise. On the day that you stand at the baptismal font, you will be handing this precious part of yourself back to God. God will be making an eternal covenant of care, claiming and adopting your child. But you have a part in this covenant too. For you will be promising to do your utmost to let the child know who and whose he or she is. You will be promising to surround your child with love in such a way that the source of love is obvious. You will be promising to be God's number one example, God's number one reflection and witness in this new, unfolding human life. This is your promise. This is your commitment.

On your own it will be impossible to keep such a promise. You may have the greatest intentions and still find that you fail. But by trusting in God's strength and living in your own baptismal covenant, by daily dying to your own sins in repentance and daily rising to a new life in the power of Christ, God will accomplish this great work in and through you.

You are making the most important commitment in your child's new life on the baptismal day. It will be a beautiful and meaningful time. But if you want it to last, make two more silent commitments at the same time.

First, recommit your life and all that you are to the Lord. Recommit yourself to being a worshiping, caring Christian who seeks out ways of service to Christ and shares His love. Recommit yourself to seeking God's will through the Word and to seeking God's wisdom, guidance, peace, and understanding for your life. Recommit your time, your talents, your treasures, and your priorities. Recommit yourself to God and ask God to mold you into the most caring Christian model of strength and goodness you can be for your child.

And second, recommit yourself to your spouse and your marriage so that, growing together in love, you can provide the most stable, secure, loving, and supportive environment possible for your child.

If you make these two commitments, you will go to the altar truly prepared to present your child to the Lord's care. And living in the covenant of your own baptism, committed to Christ and to your spouse, you will be giving your child the best chance, the best resources, the greatest gifts you could possibly give.

Thought Time

What three promises will you be making for your child at the baptismal service? (See the service in your church worship book.)

Which of these might be the hardest to keep?

What can you begin doing now that will help you keep your promises?

What promises might you want to make to each other now that will add strength to your marriage relationship?

Letter to Sponsors

TO:
FROM:
RE: THE BAPTISMAL SPONSORSHIP OF OUR CHILD

Dear Friend(s):

We know that you share in our joy at the miracle of this new birth. God has blessed us with the gift of our child and with the gift of friends like you who truly care.

Because you mean so much to us, we would like you to consider taking a special role in the life of our child. We would like you to enter into a covenant with us to serve as our child's baptismal sponsor (godparent).

Sponsorship in our church is more than just an honorary gesture. The responsibilities we expect from our child's sponsors include:

1. **To pray for our child regularly**
2. **To remember our child's baptismal anniversary and birthday every year with a card or letter**
3. **To be a model of love, care, and Christlike kindness for our child**
4. **If any thing should happen to us, to see to it that our child is brought up in the Christian faith, taught to read the Bible as a source of life and direction, and brought to worship regularly.**

We have chosen you because we believe that you, of all our friends, would sincerely try to honor this commitment and care for the spiritual well-being of our child. Please take a few days to think and pray about this commitment and let us know. We are grateful to have friends like you and will respect whatever decision you feel most comfortable with.

Love,